Daily Grace
for
Daily Life

*Our mission is to publish and distribute inspirational products offering exceptional value
and biblical encouragement to the masses.*

Member of the
Evangelical Christian
Publishers Association

Printed in China.

ENCOURAGEMENT FOR WOMEN

Daily Grace
for
Daily Life

Anita Higman & Hillary McMullen

BARBOUR
PUBLISHING

CONTENTS

Introduction

Ever since that wayward moment in Eden, we humans have been stumbling around on this fallen earth, bruised and broken in every way imaginable. But God never forgot His children. He sent us a rescuer, a supernatural hero—Jesus—who knows our fears and trials and pain. He came to illuminate our darkened souls with pure holy light and to offer us the gift of heaven.

But Jesus also cares about the here and now. He wants to have a relationship with us—including those heart-to-heart talks that offer guidance and mercy and healing. These divine blessings arrive new every day just like the manna that appeared miraculously on the desert floor for the people of Israel. So come with us and hear the whispers of heaven. Come embrace His love and light. Come gather the sustenance of God's daily grace.

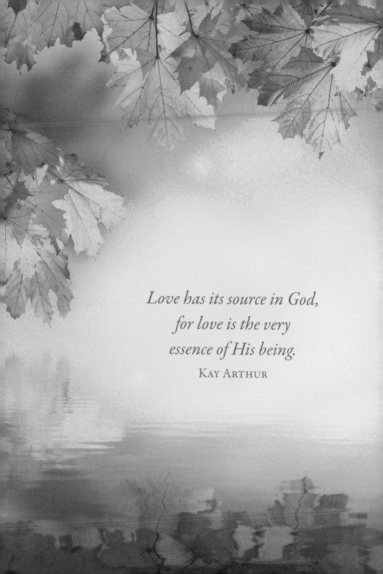

Love has its source in God,
for love is the very
essence of His being.

KAY ARTHUR

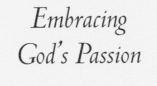

*Embracing
God's Passion*

Such Endearing Intentions

*"I led them with cords of human kindness,
with ties of love. To them I was like
one who lifts a little child to the cheek,
and I bent down to feed them."*

Hosea 11:4 niv

Throughout God's Word, He shows people the many facets of His character—His justice, His majesty, His mercy, His love. But perhaps none of the verses in the Bible are as telling of His intense passion for His beloved as when He talks of His devotion to Israel in the verse above. Since God is unchanging in nature, we know He feels this same affectionate way about His children today.

It's easy to imagine the intimate action of an earthly doting daddy lifting his child up to his face. To feel the breath of his child on his cheek. To hear the beat of her heart. To be even nearer to that precious one he loves so dearly. But what about that same scene played out with God as the Father—the holy one who people envision as unapproachable, as if He lives on the far side of a distant mountain no one can travel to? To see the God of the universe with such endearing intentions toward His creatures is too much to hope for, isn't it? And yet it was the very image that God wanted mankind to see, to know. . .to embrace. —AH

God, thank You for Your incredible tenderness and unimaginable love for me. Amen.

How Majestic Is Your Name

> LORD, our Lord, how majestic is
> your name in all the earth!
> You have set your glory in the heavens.
> PSALM 8:1 NIV

Isn't it wonderful to experience the beauty of the earth that comes from God's creative passion? For instance, the enchantment of a firefly's dance, the music of water, the gossamer mist on an alpine trail, or celestial bodies glittering on a velvet sky?

In the midst of creating, people sense a closeness to God, the ultimate designer, inventor, architect, and author. It would be impossible for them not to want to create and then gaze upward with a spirit of worship. In fact, the urgency to create can be like a full-term baby eager to be born.

That artistic life force in each human is in his or her very being, because that is the same essence found in God's character. And just as people hold up their creations to the light and pronounce them good, so does God.

To know this imaginative and passionate side of God, how can you not be changed? How can you not want to embrace God's grace through Christ so that you can be in His presence for all time? God wants to show you the place He has prepared for you—a place where His creative passion has enough surprises to last you an eternity. —AH

God, the intricacy and beauty of Your creation is astounding. Thank You for giving me the ability to create. Amen.

I Will Betroth You to Me

"I will betroth you to me forever;
I will betroth you in righteousness and justice,
in love and compassion."

HOSEA 2:19 NIV

Everybody enjoys a wedding. God must love weddings, too. The Bible is full of references to them, including the Lord referring to Himself as the bridegroom. One instance when God connects Himself to the imagery of brides-and grooms-to-be is in the book of Hosea. The Almighty says, "I will betroth you to me forever." He's not just referring to the nation of Israel here, but to you personally. Betrothed doesn't come up a lot in modern conversation, but people still get strong impressions from the word.

When God created mankind, it was a little like an arranged marriage. God had hoped the first couple would want to enjoy intimate and sweet fellowship with Him for all time. He never meant for Adam and Eve to be torn from the walks and talks they enjoyed with Him in the cool of the evening. God intended to love them and watch over them, but the first couple—Adam and Eve—opted to divorce God through their sinful choice. A prideful decision, which every person has made since then.

The "happily ever after" news in the midst of this separation is that there can be reconciliation, through Christ. The bridegroom awaits your answer. Will you take His hand? —AH

God, I want to be reunited with You. Please be my lifelong companion. Amen.

The Hound of Heaven

"If a man owns a hundred sheep, and one of them wanders away, will he not leave the ninety-nine on the hills and go to look for the one that wandered off? And if he finds it, truly I tell you, he is happier about that one sheep than about the ninety-nine that did not wander off. In the same way your Father in heaven is not willing that any of these little ones should perish."

MATTHEW 18:12–14 NIV

Just as God is passionate about His creatures, so is He passionate about the redemption of their fallen state. Jesus' desire is that no man or woman should perish, so He will go after you like a shepherd searching tirelessly for his lost sheep. There is no lamb so lost that He cannot find it, no sin so ensnaring that He cannot free the lamb from its trap.

In the poem "The Hound of Heaven," Francis Thompson wrote how God will lovingly pursue every living soul even when they flee from Him and hide:

I sped. . .
From those strong Feet that followed,
followed after.
But with unhurrying chase,
And unperturbèd pace,
Deliberate speed, majestic instancy,
They beat. . . .

Yes, God is the ever-loving shepherd searching for you, the ever-chasing hound of heaven pursuing you, because more than anything He wants to love, redeem, and cherish you. Will you let God catch you? —AH

God, I'm thankful that
Your love relentlessly pursues me. Amen.

An Everlasting Love

The LORD appeared to us in the past, saying:
"I have loved you with an everlasting love;
I have drawn you with unfailing kindness."
JEREMIAH 31:3 NIV

This world is fallen—fractured. Try picturing an exquisite hand-blown ball made of flawless crystal, rolling perilously down a hill, and then imagine all that beauty shattering into a thousand pieces. That's our earth when it fell. Not much left but scraps of glory found in the rubble of what's left of God's masterwork— which was to be a timeless creation of resplendent grandeur inhabited by perfect, free-willed creatures.

Knowing about the earth's destruction and yearning for its restoration can make its inhabitants lose heart. Every day people rummage around in the debris of what was once whole and beautiful, trying to piece together some semblance of that paradise lost. The enemy would like nothing better than for you to be so disheartened and despondent that you start to mistrust the one who made the earth, not the one who encouraged its fall. But that persuasion is as evil and as perilous as Adam and Eve's disobedience in the garden. God's love for His creatures is still as resplendent and timeless as His original creation. Never forget. Never lose heart in the one who made the beauty. Flee from the one who came to destroy it. —AH

God, when I see suffering and injustice in the world, help me not to distrust or blame You. You bring restoration. Amen.

With Great Love

*We were ready to share with you not only
the gospel of God but also our own selves,
because you had become very dear to us.*

1 THESSALONIANS 2:8 ESV

Overconfidence in one's opinions can sometimes
make that person prideful, narrow-minded, and
disrespectful of the beliefs of others. As possessors
of biblical truth, Christians must avoid this attitude.
Spreading the gospel is more than winning an
argument, proving a point, or spouting biblical
knowledge. Believers should be able to listen to the
views, concerns, and questions of others without
lashing out in anger or pride.

Evangelism cannot be done without love and
great respect. If there is no genuine care for the
person, a Christian's words lose their impact and
worth. The gospel is best presented through

a believer's attitude and lifestyle—in random kindness to friends, strangers, and enemies and in having an unearthly joy and peace in circumstances that would normally cause anxiety or frustration.

True evangelism is much more than repeating key verses and doctrines; it's sharing pieces of yourself and being open, vulnerable, and honest so that others feel free to do the same. It's extending grace and patience where it's least deserved because we have received the same loving treatment from our Savior. It is only then that a Christian is spreading the gospel in its purest form. —HM

God, above all, help me to love. That is the surest way of sharing the good news. Amen.

Deeper Bonds

May the God of endurance and encouragement grant you to live in such harmony with one another, in accord with Christ Jesus, that together you may with one voice glorify the God and Father of our Lord Jesus Christ.

ROMANS 15:5–6 ESV

It's tempting for Christians to want their church friends to see them only in their Sunday best. To be glimpsed once a week with a Bible in their hand and a smile on their face. Depression, doubt, and struggles with sin aren't generally the topics discussed after the service. As a result, Christians are forced to maintain the illusion that they are perfectly put together and in control.

However, putting on this facade makes for superficial friendships with fellow Christians. Those relationships lack honesty and vulnerability. Life can be a lonely, difficult road without empathy, wise counsel, and genuine fellowship. Because Christians share their beliefs and purpose, their bond can be made all the stronger by uniting under the same banner and encouraging one another to make a greater impact for the kingdom. The body of Christ is strengthened not by weak and shallow relationships but by forming a deep understanding of one another, loving in spite of sin, and supporting each other in gaining a closer walk with God. —HM

God, help me to be open with fellow believers and to be an encouragement to others. Amen.

A God of Many Facets

This is love: not that we loved God, but that he loved us and sent his Son as an atoning sacrifice for our sins.
1 John 4:10 niv

Trying to visualize God can be close to impossible. Often, the image that comes to mind is of a man with a silver beard and hard eyes, leaning over the edge of the clouds and ruling over his subjects with detached austerity.

This picture gives one the sense that God is stoic and indifferent to His creation. However, God created the whole colorful spectrum of human emotions, and just as the people He created are multifaceted, so is He. Throughout the Bible, God shows anger, delight, sadness, compassion, joy, patience, kindness, and tenderness. He even yearns jealously for His people when they turn to idols. He created laughter, creativity, and the bonds between good friends.

And greatest of all, in His desire to reunite humans with Himself, God sent His only Son to earth to die for their sins and redeem them. Because of this, it is plain that God does not reign unconcerned and uninvolved from His heavenly throne but instead has a character brimming with mercy and love. —HM

God, Your love is unfathomable.
Thank You for Your Son. Amen.

Defying Apathy

So, because you are lukewarm, and neither hot nor cold, I will spit you out of my mouth.
REVELATION 3:16 ESV

Apathy is a stealthy foe. It can overtake even the most zealous people, numbing them in slow, almost imperceptible degrees, prompting their passion to fade into a half-hearted pursuit and, in time, hardening into a cold, uncaring lethargy.

Unfortunately, Christians are just as susceptible to the disease of indifference in their relationship with God. Sermons begin to repeat themselves, Bible verses lose their impact, worship becomes less moving, and prayers go unanswered. When Christians start to lose sight of the wonder and depth of Jesus' grace and saving power, all the duties and activities surrounding the lifestyle will become dry and lose their joy. The foundation of their faith will be weakened, causing the house built above it to buckle and sway.

But God calls us to be deliriously in love with Him. He wants us to yearn for Him, desiring Him above all else. Like a fire that needs fuel, our relationship with God requires care and watchfulness. When the flames begin to burn low, we must take action and cry out to Him, trusting that He'll answer. To combat apathy, we must never forget the priceless treasure we have found in Jesus. —HM

God, help my passion for You to always be growing. To glorify You is my purpose and my greatest end. Amen.

I never knew how to worship
until I knew how to love.

HENRY WARD BEECHER

Practicing the Art of Praise

An Exquisite Tribute

Shout for joy to the LORD, all the earth. Worship the LORD with gladness; come before him with joyful songs. Know that the LORD is God. It is he who made us, and we are his; we are his people, the sheep of his pasture. Enter his gates with thanksgiving and his courts with praise; give thanks to him and praise his name. For the LORD is good and his love endures forever; his faithfulness continues through all generations.

PSALM 100:1–5 NIV

The book of Psalms contains some pretty heavy expressions of lament and cries to God for help, but it also includes many beautiful prayers and hymns, which make an exquisite tribute to the Almighty. They include the words *gladness*, *joyful*, *thanksgiving*, and *praise*. It is good and right to take these psalms from your hearts to your lips.

In fact, reading one of these psalms out loud in the morning is a perfect way to start the day. Bagels and coffee are good, but the psalms will nourish your soul. It will give you a reverent connection with the Lord, set a joyful tone for the day, and offer you a powerful way to worship God in spirit and in truth. —AH

God, give me a grateful heart and help me not to overlook all the blessings that You've given me and all the ways You've loved me. Amen.

A Thank You to Heaven

One of them, when he saw he was healed, came back, praising God in a loud voice. He threw himself at Jesus' feet and thanked him—and he was a Samaritan. Jesus asked, "Were not all ten cleansed? Where are the other nine? Has no one returned to give praise to God except this foreigner?"
LUKE 17:15–19 NIV

When a child is given a gift, many times parents will coax her into an appreciative response by asking, "So, what do you say?" Obviously the answer is, "Thank you." Mom and Dad are trying to teach their children good manners. They want their kids to grow up with a thankful heart and not with the belief that they deserve every good thing without even considering the sacrifice and feelings of the giver.

Even Jesus would like a thank you for His gifts. In the Bible, when ten men were healed from leprosy and all but one went on their way without coming back to thank Jesus, He asked, "Where are the other nine?"

That's a pretty heartbreaking situation. So it looks like parents are right after all. A grateful heart is a good way to handle life, and the words *thank you* are enjoyed by everyone, including God. What can you thank the Lord for this day, this very moment? —AH

God, thank You for Your
sacrifice and provision. Amen.

Evil Will Not Prevail

For our struggle is not against flesh and blood, but against the rulers, against the authorities, against the powers of this dark world and against the spiritual forces of evil in the heavenly realms.

Ephesians 6:12 niv

Because of man's disobedience, our world is shadowed with darkness and riddled with evil. Even Christians, struggling with the consequences of sinful choices and with spiritual forces, are not exempt from trouble. How can people deal with attacks from the spiritual realm?

One way is to praise God *through* the sorrows. Doing so will strengthen us on the deepest level, even though, at times, it feels like the hardest thing ever asked of us.

Praise not only contains power but also serves as a battle cry. Christians can assume that when trouble comes, there are opposing forces at work. Satan and his demons do not want anyone to raise his or her voice in thanksgiving. They hate all forms of worship that bring honor to God and weaken the dark side's position. But that shouldn't stop anyone from giving God His glory. After all, the forces of evil will not prevail, and in the end, God wins. Praise God! —AH

God, there is no reason to fear with You by my side. Nothing can overpower You. Amen

A Life Lived in Praise

*May these words of my mouth and this
meditation of my heart be pleasing in your
sight, LORD, my Rock and my Redeemer.*
PSALM 19:14 NIV

Sing God's praises even when you don't feel like
it. A backache, a hurtful remark, a job layoff, a
breakup, a devastating illness, a death in the family.
All of these troubles along life's road can make a
worshipful attitude seem difficult. Even impossible.
But when people follow through with praise in spite
of their feelings, a new spirit will emerge.

Additionally, praise is not just in one's song
or words or hands lifted to the heavens. A whole
life can be lived in praise. In choosing peace over
conflict. Forgiveness over bitterness. Humility over
pride. Love over hate. All of these daily choices are a

form of praise, because they honor God's way—they are choices that bring heaven to earth, even if only for a moment. Let the prayer of your heart be, "May these words of my mouth and this meditation of my heart be pleasing in your sight, Lord, my Rock and my Redeemer." —AH

God, even when I'm in the midst of trials, I want my thoughts, words, and actions to point to You and bring You glory. Amen.

No Wrong Way to Worship

Great is the LORD, and greatly to be praised,
and his greatness is unsearchable.
PSALM 145:3 ESV

Worship can at times be an uncomfortable experience. Clapping may feel awkward and forced. There are high notes in some hymns that only the bravest sopranos can reach. Are worshippers always supposed to raise their hands, sing at the top of their lungs, and be emotionally moved by the music? Some Sunday mornings, even the most well-intentioned worshippers may feel like a dry well, believing they have nothing to offer in praise. Christians young and old can fall into this trap, glancing at their neighbors during the song, wondering how their voices can sound so earnest when they themselves can barely squeeze out a word. But Christians shouldn't have to feel self-conscious during worship.

The purpose of musical worship isn't about singing artificial praise or responding to music like everyone else. It's about becoming humble before God and appreciating all He's done. Every person has a unique way of coming to God. Some may love to sing loudly with eyes squeezed shut. Others may study the lyrics, remembering how the truths have been manifested in their lives. Worship is incredibly natural when the focus is placed on God and not on how we may appear to others. —HM

God, teach me how to praise You in a genuine way and without fear. You are worthy. Amen.

Grocery List Prayers

"Pray like this: 'Our Father in heaven,
Your name is holy.'"
MATTHEW 6:9 NLV

Sometimes, prayers can begin to sound like bulleted grocery lists. It's an incredibly easy habit to fall into. There is always quite a handful of relatives, friends, and acquaintances with health problems or dire circumstances. Then there is the complex web of personal issues—emotional, physical, and spiritual. By the time the prayer is finally wrapped up, one might have the sense that she has just checked off a box on her to-do list, and now it's time to crawl into bed or send the kids off to school. This ritual may become a monotonous rut that becomes difficult to climb out of.

While Jesus was on earth, He gave brief instructions on how to pray. Before He recited a single need, Jesus started His prayer with praise by calling God's name holy. It requires patience to praise before listing petitions. It also requires a shift in perspective. The focus of the prayer is transferred from ourselves to the might, magnificence, and magnitude of God. Instead of feeling loaded down with the sheer volume of requests, we can revel in the fact that He is in control and much greater than our problems. —HM

God, You are faithful and steadfast.
May my praise be pleasing to You. Amen.

Joyful Labor

Whatever work you do, do it with all your heart.
Do it for the Lord and not for men.
COLOSSIANS 3:23 NLV

For some people, work is drudgery. They are blinded to all else but the slow hands of the clock, ticking away the seconds until their next break. For others, work could just be something they do to pass the time. They might feel their occupation is insignificant and trivial. There's a certain hopelessness that comes when one's life is dominated by burdensome or tedious work, compelling some weary laborers to doubt their own purpose.

Yet work can be so much more. For those committed to glorifying God through their daily actions, a simple or tiring occupation suddenly becomes worthwhile and significant. The scope of their work expands to showing Christ to those around them and having a joyful heart in all they do, all the while being firm in the realization that God is with them every step of the way. This type of work, saturated in trust and love for God, is a form of worship. God can use occupations great and small for His glory, and when we worship Him in our daily lives, He will give us the joy and strength to accomplish anything. —HM

God, please help me to remember that work is not meant to be painful or dreary but a means to worship and glorify You. Amen.

Praise in the Present

This is the day that the LORD has made;
let us rejoice and be glad in it.
PSALM 118:24 ESV

Two of the largest burdens to carry are shame from the past and fear of the future. Like a game of tug of war, clinging to sin pulls people back to painful memories and feelings of guilt, while harboring anxiety for the days to come drags them relentlessly onward, tearing their attention away from the present.

But we were designed to live out a greater purpose than merely straining under the weight of past wrongs and upcoming trials. Being unable to enjoy the existing moment because one's mind and heart are overburdened is to be denied one of God's greatest gifts to humanity. He gave people senses so that they could appreciate His creation.

He gifted them with the ability to create, love, and worship. The present was made to be rejoiced in and experienced fully. There is no joy or progress in bitterness and worry.

When we trust in the grace of Christ to wipe away our sins, and put Him in control of our future, we are able to turn our eyes to the infinite opportunities of the present. There is always beauty to be found, people to be loved, and chances to praise God. —HM

God, I am redeemed and You are in control. Help me to live in the present with joy in my heart and praise on my lips. Amen.

Singing in the Rain

*But I am afflicted and in pain; let your
salvation, O God, set me on high! I will
praise the name of God with a song;
I will magnify him with thanksgiving.*
PSALM 69:29–30 ESV

It's easy to praise God when the sun is up, the sky
is clear, and all is well. There are those occasional
moments in life when one feels weightless and at
peace with the world. The light seems brighter,
the trees more beautiful, and a cup of coffee
more delicious. And perhaps circumstances
have lined up perfectly to allow a brief period
of worship and thankfulness to God. But these
blissful moments when heaven seems to bend a
little closer to the earth can be scarce. If believers
wait for these rare scraps of time to lift their
voices or thoughts in praise, their offerings of
adoration may be few.

David wrote many of his psalms during periods of great emotional turmoil and physical danger. Yet his writings include incredibly moving passages of praise, awe, and thanksgiving given to God, even when David's enemies relentlessly pursued him and life dealt one blow after another. Despite the storms he weathered, David remembered the magnitude and loving-kindness of his God and praised him continually.
—HM

God, help me to remember You in times of distress and discomfort. May my praise be beautiful to Your ears. Amen.

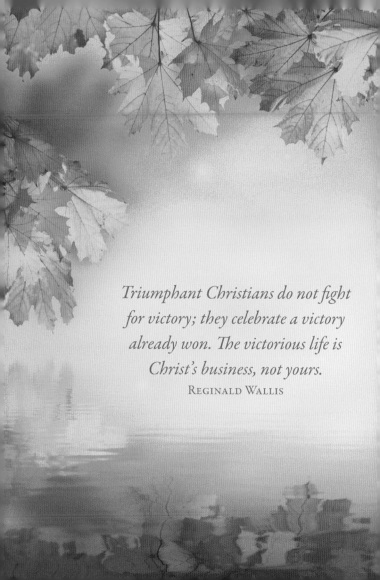

Triumphant Christians do not fight for victory; they celebrate a victory already won. The victorious life is Christ's business, not yours.

REGINALD WALLIS

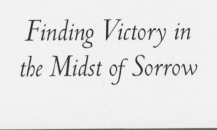

*Finding Victory in
the Midst of Sorrow*

Rejoicing Comes in the Morning

Weeping may stay for the night,
but rejoicing comes in the morning.
<small>PSALM 30:5 NIV</small>

Victory over pain and sorrow doesn't mean ignoring it. God doesn't expect people to stub their toe on the coffee table and merely come up smiling. Unfortunately, pain is a part of life. The only healthy and realistic way to deal with pain and suffering is to first acknowledge them. Lean into them if need be. But never walk away and say they mean nothing. Being alive is tricky and tough in a thousand different ways, and the pain is as real as the throbbing red toe attached to the foot that smacks that table leg in the middle of the night.

Where can one go once pain has been experienced? Well, that's where God comes in. He doesn't leave His children high and dry. He made promises that He will lead His precious ones—you—to green pastures and to waters so still one can hear the very voice of God. There in that place, just you and God—He will give you rest from the weary world. Ask Him, and He will draw near. Dawn does break through the dark gloom of night. Peace can be regained. And then rejoicing is not far behind. —AH

———————————————

God, help me to put my hope in You
in times of both peace and turmoil.
I trust in Your promises. Amen.

I Have Called You Friends

"I no longer call you servants, because a servant does not know his master's business. Instead, I have called you friends, for everything that I learned from my Father I have made known to you."
JOHN 15:15 NIV

Most of us have heard the old saying that people are like islands. Even with thousands of friends on various online social networks, the sensation of aloneness can be sharp and real. Lonesomeness is easy to feel, since people are moving faster and faster and have shorter and shorter attention spans. If people are becoming more isolated, what can be done?

Remember that humans were not meant to go it alone. Cultivating good solid friendships is time-consuming but valuable. Friends can provide the soft landing when life drops you without a parachute.

If you find yourself in short supply of friends, know that Jesus has called you His friend. There is no one who is better qualified to be a friend than the one who made you. He will carry you across an ocean of despair and through a desert of loneliness. Victory in the midst of sorrow is easier with a friend at your side, especially when His name is Jesus.
—AH

God, thank You for calling me friend.
When I feel alone, help me cling to You. Amen.

We Were Created for Love

Even though I walk through the darkest valley,
I will fear no evil, for you are with me;
your rod and your staff, they comfort me.
PSALM 23:4 NIV

We were created to embrace love, imagination, peace, and beauty and to enjoy a close relationship with God, not to be filled with hate and grief. Just as a car was never meant to run on muddy water, our spirits were never meant to live in sorrow. Even though God knew man would fall into disobedience if he were given freewill, the human soul was never meant to know sin's barren landscape—nor to feel its brutal force.

God did not leave us in the shadow of death with no comfort. He sent His Son to wash away all sin like a garment made clean. Yes, even though you may walk through the darkest valley, there's no need to fear evil, for the Lord is with you. Christ makes victory possible, now and forevermore. He offers a gift of forgiveness and eternal life so that His creatures may once again be allowed to enter a paradise lost—where we can once again embrace love, imagination, peace, and beauty and all the delights that come from a close relationship with God. —AH

God, through You I can experience a perfect love. The world dims in comparison to You. Amen.

Soaring on Wings of Eagles

*But those who hope in the LORD will renew
their strength. They will soar on wings like
eagles; they will run and not grow weary,
they will walk and not be faint.*

ISAIAH 40:31 NIV

Everyone wants to be filled with hope—to soar on
wings like eagles. What an image. To fly free from
troubles and leave all one's cares so far behind that
they become no more than a faded spot on the
horizon or a distant memory. But what happens
when that hope doesn't arrive right away and
despair settles in? Perhaps it means that the search
for hope has been in all the wrong places.

The world's courage and faith and promises are counterfeit. Man-made hope—a hope without God—will bring as much warmth as a lake of ice, and it will be as real and satisfying as a bowl of plastic fruit.

The book of Isaiah says to hope in the Lord; He will renew your strength. As you cling to that truth, expect a miracle. You will indeed soar on wings like eagles. —AH

God, help me not to cling to a flimsy, temporal hope but to look to You for my deliverance and sustenance. Your grace has set me free. Amen.

No More Than We Can Bear

God is faithful; he will not let you be
tempted beyond what you can bear.
But when you are tempted, he will also
provide a way out so that you can endure it.
1 CORINTHIANS 10:13 NIV

Temptations come in many forms. They are not always dressed in lurid clothes or lurking in darkened alleyways. For instance, a temptation might be to indulge in bitterness while calling it righteous indignation. Being angry with circumstances is a natural reaction, but to be angry with God and allow it to fester into bitterness can result in the same devastating folly that comes from more obvious sins.

The world's pull is powerful, and even misdirected sorrow can play right into the enemy's hands. Knowing Satan's ploys is the first step in undoing those raised fists before God and turning them into raised hands of praise.

Take comfort in the scriptures that promise the Lord's faithfulness. God won't allow anyone to be tempted beyond what she can bear. But when temptation comes—even if it's the lure of anger-laden grief directed at the Almighty— know that God will also provide a way out of the temptation so that it can be endured. Draw comfort in trusting the true heart of God. —AH

God, help me to keep my eyes open to Satan's ploys and give me the strength and wisdom to resist them. Amen.

The Beauty of Brokenness

For the sake of Christ, then, I am content with
weaknesses, insults, hardships, persecutions, and
calamities. For when I am weak, then I am strong.
2 Corinthians 12:10 esv

Imprisonment. A shipwreck. Beatings. A deadly snakebite. These are just a few of the hardships Paul endured on his journey to spread the Good News. The most amazing thing is that he didn't just drag himself through his trials with a heavy heart or a protesting mind; he remained content through it all.

The reason for Paul's perseverance and faithfulness is that he constantly relied upon God's strength in his weakness. Paul was not disillusioned into thinking he could bear the pain and danger of his persecutions alone, bolstered by nothing but his own human spirit. His complete dependence on the protection and grace of God gave him supernatural strength. Paul attained victory through Christ not just *in spite* of his weakness but *because* of his weakness and trust in his Savior.

Many Christians today might find these kinds of trials difficult to relate to, but Paul sets a wonderful example. Whatever anyone's afflictions may be, there is victory in acknowledging one's own weakness and trusting in God. —HM

God, no matter what I'm going through, help me to realize I can't do it alone. You are my strength. Amen.

The Little Things

*Whatever is good and perfect comes
down to us from God our Father,
who created all the lights in the heavens.*
JAMES 1:17 NLT

One of the best ways to shrug off a bad mood is to start noticing the little things. It may take a Herculean effort to see past the frustrations and annoyances that can pile up during the day, but when the shift of focus is made, sunshine pierces the gloom.

Despite all the darkness some days can bring, God has provided a blanket of mercies that will cushion the fall. These mercies become visible when the downtrodden and exhausted deliberately pause in the midst of their fast-paced, distracted lives and remove the blinders obstructing their view, revealing a vast amount of blessings given to them by a doting Father.

These can range from a friend's faithfulness to the comfort of a favorite armchair, from a good meal to an uplifting book.

These may seem like everyday, commonplace pleasures, but they are also tiny helping hands supporting us through the harshness and insensitivity of life. And, of course, the greatest consolation that will shield us from every injustice is the victory we have through Jesus Christ. This assurance can vanquish the worst of moods. —HM

God, thank You for taking such wonderful care of me. Amen.

One Sip at a Time

God is our refuge and strength, a very present help in trouble. Therefore we will not fear though the earth gives way, though the mountains be moved into the heart of the sea, though its waters roar and foam, though the mountains tremble at its swelling.

PSALM 46:1–3 ESV

Grief leaves no one unvisited. It passes like a shadow, shading one's world with gloom and despair. Grief can seem to stretch on forever, unsurpassable and always present. Every future hope is extinguished, and it seems as if no joy will ever be able to penetrate the darkness again.

Bone-deep anguish can't be swallowed whole. Like a scalding cup of tea, if gulped down, it will sear and blister. The only bearable way to consume it is one miniscule sip at a time. If the mourner decides to live minute by minute, hour by hour, day by day, leaving the weight of the future in God's capable hands and asking Him for comfort in the present, she will be sustained. God's power can reach into the deepest depths of despair. And in time, be it months or years, the burning cup of grief will cool, and life will be sweet to the tongue again, ready to be savored. —HM

---

*God, You are my comfort
in the darkest times. Amen.*

Embracing Hardship

*When troubles come your way, consider
it an opportunity for great joy. For you
know that when your faith is tested,
your endurance has a chance to grow.*

JAMES 1:2–3 NLT

Trials are unavoidable, whether it's frustrations
with work, anxiety about children, or loss of
a loved one. Generally, trials are viewed as
obstacles interrupting the regular flow of life,
causing pain, stress, or depression. It is natural to
abhor suffering in its every form, to want to find
a place without sorrow or discomfort.

However, James told his fellow Christians to
find joy in tribulation because it strengthened their
faith and endurance. He believed that through
trials, people would be forced to seek God more
fervently than in times of peace. In the center of

—66—

our misery, we are able to experience firsthand God's saving power, refining our character and increasing our reliance on Christ.

It seems unnatural to embrace suffering as a tutor, to learn from it willingly and seek its benefits. But God can use trials to draw people to Himself when they realize life cannot be lived on their own power. When the sufferer finally emerges from the darkness of her agony, she will find herself on a higher plane and closer to God's heart. —HM

God, when I'm in the throes of misfortune, help me to remember that You are in control. I want to find joy in all circumstances. Amen.

The Cross He Bore

"In the world you will have tribulation.
But take heart; I have overcome the world."
JOHN 16:33 ESV

Imagine slowly awakening to the realization
that God has marked you for a monumental
yet agonizing purpose: to surrender yourself to
a brutal and undeserved death in order to save
humanity. This lot fell to Jesus during His time on
earth. He experienced overwhelming tribulations,
temptations, and cause for doubt and fear in His
short life. He encountered disbelief, hatred, and
persecution from those He sought to redeem.

Yet despite the incredible and unfathomable
difficulty of His task, Jesus conquered sin and death.

In His ministry, He reached out to the rejected and offered healing to the sick and hopeless. Jesus accomplished these things through a total reliance on His Father. Because of His commitment and passionate love for God, He abstained from a life of normalcy and comfort to carry out His mission.

Just as Jesus was supported by a close communion with God, so can we draw strength, nourishment, and fulfillment from an intimate association with Jesus. When we face trials and sorrows, Christ has encouraged us to take heart because He has already won the ultimate victory.
—HM

God, my help comes from You. Thank You for being greater than my troubles. Amen.

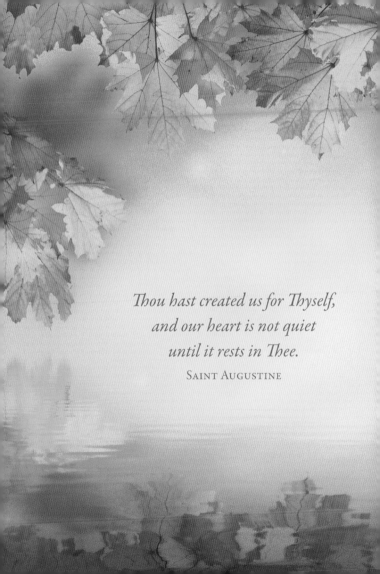

Thou hast created us for Thyself,
and our heart is not quiet
until it rests in Thee.

SAINT AUGUSTINE

Decluttering Our Spirits

The Baggage of the Soul

Do not conform to the pattern of this world, but be transformed by the renewing of your mind. Then you will be able to test and approve what God's will is.

ROMANS 12:2 NIV

People declutter their closets, their dirty garages, and their messy drawers, but what about their soul? A good question to ask is, "What is it that holds me back from living free of the spiritual baggage of unforgiveness, pride, envy, idolatry, and strife?" Wouldn't it be wonderful to cut that load loose and rise up to find that your legs were meant for running, your heart for laughing, and your spirit for lightness?

That kind of spiritual liberty can be yours by not conforming to the morality of this world but instead allowing Christ to renew your mind, bringing you a clearer discernment of God's good, pleasing, and perfect will.

Spiritual decluttering is a little like hitting the REFRESH button on one's computer—you get to start all over with a new day, full of hours that haven't been muddled with fumbling, failure, and transgression. Such a renewal translates into a life that fits you well—a beautiful and useful one that God envisioned when you were first created. —AH

God, cleanse my spirit and mind and make me receptive to Your perfect will. Amen.

Rubbed the Wrong Way!

Get rid of all bitterness, rage and anger, brawling and slander, along with every form of malice. Be kind and compassionate to one another, forgiving each other, just as in Christ God forgave you.
EPHESIANS 4:31–32 NIV

It's easy to get offended in this life. Because of misunderstandings, painful memories, different points of view, diverse backgrounds and cultures, people's fleshly impulses, and a host of other reasons, it's common to come away from a conversation feeling slighted, snubbed, or out-and-out insulted. What are we to do?

Sometimes it's a matter of getting out of the "always offended rut" by choosing not to be hypersensitive to people's bad manners and conduct. Yes, people really *do* say thoughtless things. They are as real as the thoughtless things *you've* said when provoked. Everyone has done it, including Christians. No one is exempt. But to live in a constant state of offend-ability will only cause grief, not to mention chronic stomach troubles! If you find yourself feeling slighted and angry, tell God about it, and then let it go. Let Him handle it. Forgive whomever needs forgiving, knowing you, too, will be in need of that same mercy soon enough. —AH

God, give me patience and compassion in my dealings with others. Help me to extend forgiveness wherever it's due. Amen.

The World Is Notorious

*I can do all this through
him who gives me strength.*
PHILIPPIANS 4:13 NIV

The world is notorious for getting things backward. It calls good, evil, and darkness, light. And so it is with strength and weakness. Little children are told not to cry, but to grow up and to be strong. The world believes that to be human is to be godlike, autonomous, the master of one's destiny. But, in reality, those beliefs are falsehoods. They have the shadows of darkness surrounding them because they are whispers emanating from the father of lies.

So, with the help of the world, children grow up to be seemingly "self-sufficient." But in reality, they are frail in body, mind, and spirit. God alone gives us strength for each day, every hour—literally for every breath we take. Through Christ, people have the capacity to do great things, to be noble and to rise above all that is unholy on this earth. What a paradox, that when we are humbled and weak in ourselves, we are the most powerful in God—and yet it is simplicity itself. We can do all things through Christ, who gives us strength. With Him, nothing is impossible. Amen! —AH

God, I am weak and hopeless without You. Help me to trust in Your strength. Amen.

When It's All About You

Pride goes before destruction,
a haughty spirit before a fall.
PROVERBS 16:18 NIV

Pride is a bottomless lake of arrogance, and the streams and rivers that feed it come from just about everywhere. The world would love for people to believe that being front and center in life is always better than working quietly behind the scenes. That the heroes and role models in this world are the stars of stage, screen, and sports.

Ralph Waldo Emerson said, "Most of the shadows of life are caused by standing in our own sunshine." Great quote, right? When people are busy "shining" and "whirling" through life, they rarely see the shadows they make or the lives that could have been changed if they had spent a little less time pursuing the limelight and a little more time making themselves available to God. There is power in a life well-lived according to God's plan. Not the kind of power of celebrity-hood, but the kind that leads to redemption and love. The kind that will change the world, one soul at a time. —AH

God, there is much more to life than bringing glory to myself. Help me to shift my focus to You and others. Amen.

Window Shopping

*Be happy in the Lord. And He
will give you the desires of your heart.*
PSALM 37:4 NLV

Window shopping can at times be more bitter
than sweet. The average person cannot possibly
buy all the beautiful and tantalizing things that the
world has to offer. Yet many women fall prey to the
insatiable desire to have more and more.

However, the need for more can go beyond the
material. It can extend to obtaining the right career
opportunities, a flawless appearance, or a stress-
free environment. The shopper, desperate in her
search for perfection, glances wildly through shop
windows with covetous eyes. If she does acquire one
of the presumably precious gifts, there is a moment
of elation as she cradles and admires it.

But maintaining lasting happiness on one's own takes a heavy toll. Eventually, the shopper will find a flaw previously overlooked on the surface of the item. When its luster fades, she'll be back to peeking through the glass, aching for the new and better piece that is sure to complete the puzzle. To end the cycle, we must trust that God knows exactly what gift we need and when it should be given. Window shopping will lead only to temporal happiness and dissatisfaction, but trusting God will result in contentedness and eternal happiness. —HM

God, I trust that You know what
I need better than I do. Amen.

To Worry Is to Waste

"Therefore do not be anxious about tomorrow,
for tomorrow will be anxious for itself."
MATTHEW 6:34 ESV

Anxious hearts rarely find comfort or peace.
Always flitting about from one problem to the
next, they can never pause and enjoy the beauty
of a blooming rosebush or the warmth of a cup
of tea.

Unfortunately, anxiety is a common malady,
riding on the coattails of unpaid bills, flighty
husbands, disobedient children, or unstable
jobs. Like a silent thief, it steals away the joys of
a fresh morning and pushes all the problems of
life—big and small—into the forefront of the
victim's mind.

Escaping anxiety can be close to impossible—unless Jesus' words of hope become a reality. While He was on earth, He told His listeners to drive the worries of tomorrow from their minds. He wanted them to revel in the richness and provision of the present day. But it almost seems irresponsible. Competent and self-sufficient women naturally recoil from the idea of surrendering their schedules, to-do lists, worries, and problems. But Jesus calls for trust and surrender, which, although seemingly scary, brings exquisite relief. —HM

God, please help me to surrender all of the burdens I carry daily. You are infinitely more capable. Amen.

Standing in Shadow

A tranquil heart gives life to the flesh,
but envy makes the bones rot.
PROVERBS 14:30 ESV

Everyone knows *that* woman. Perfect hair, beautiful singing voice, a brain for business, immaculate homemaker, life of the party, and, of course, she extends compassion to those who need it. It's almost sickening. When other women encounter her, they might feel as though they're standing in an immense shadow. Next to her, their light feels dimmer, their achievements smaller, their appearance inferior, and their personality dryer.

When women compare themselves to a star that seems to shine brighter, being who they are no longer seems special or significant. Why try to accomplish anything if someone else can do it better?

But God has created each person with unique gifts and a specific purpose. He has given His children the tools they need in order to bring glory to Him. A person's faithfulness is not measured by what she is given, but what she *does* with what she is given. When we have envy in our hearts against others who we think are more capable and gifted, we're overlooking and wasting the blessings God has given us. —HM

God, help me not to compare myself to others but to shine as Your unique creation. Amen.

Idol Factories

Dear children, keep yourselves from idols.
1 JOHN 5:21 NIV

Humans were created to worship. According to John Calvin, the human heart is a factory of idols. Spanning from ancient history to present day, mankind has constantly manufactured false deities in their desperation to fulfill the God-given desire to revere and pay homage to something, hoping that the object of their blind devotion will dole out a shred of happiness and security. However, the refuge they seek in the arms of these unfeeling, unforgiving gods is nonexistent, despite faithful and costly sacrifices at the feet of these idols.

Whatever it is that we have placed upon a pedestal, whether it is money, a romantic relationship, success, or our own comfort, it will never satisfy the needs that can only be provided for by our Creator. If His children place their trust entirely upon Him and finally grasp the insufficiency of all other sources to sustain and protect them through life, God will remain exalted. The supreme function of the human heart is to worship and adore God. When we worship Him alone, we are carrying out our greatest purpose—one filled with love and joy.

—HM

God, help me to cast aside anything that I might be placing ahead of You. You are my ultimate provider and stronghold. Amen.

Citadel of Self-Sufficiency

*"Come to me, all who labor and are
heavy laden, and I will give you rest."*
MATTHEW 11:28 ESV

To stay upright in the swirling madness of careers,
spouses, children, and daily tasks, women have to be
strong. They have to remain focused and in control.

When these principles have been firmly planted
into a woman's psyche, she begins to build up a
stronghold in her mind, based on pride and self-
sufficiency. She equips herself to take on the world
alone, firm in her resolve. However, this attitude
isolates her from the kindness of others and from
the only strength that can sustain her—God's.

Eventually, her fortress will come under a siege of trials and frustrations that not even the fiercest of women could conquer. Broken and at wit's end, she can either accept help or stay miserable, huddled beside the remains of her citadel.

When she finally grasps God's outstretched hand and relies on *His* strength, there is joyful release and beautiful humility in the surrender. One could almost feel a certain return to the sweet dependency of childhood, trusting in a greater force to care for her problems, and giving others the opportunity to swoop in, making a solitary, wearisome life rich and blissfully free. —HM

God, don't allow me to become so wrapped up in life that I forget Your provision and joy. Amen.

What does love look like? It has the hands to help others. It has the feet to hasten to the poor and needy. It has eyes to see misery and want. It has the ears to hear the sighs and sorrows of men. That is what love looks like.

Saint Augustine

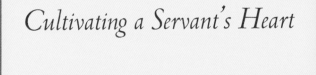

Cultivating a Servant's Heart

An Impossible Way to Live

"His master replied, 'Well done, good and faithful servant! You have been faithful with a few things; I will put you in charge of many things. Come and share your master's happiness!'"

MATTHEW 25:21 NIV

College graduates expect their dream job the day after they receive their diploma, and newlyweds hope to have a house even before the words "I do" have faded from their lips. Humans have never been too good at waiting on things. People generally want what they want when they want it. Period. It's as if all members of humanity are holding their breath, waiting until they have everything they've ever wanted before they will breathe. Or live. Or serve.

But God wants us to be content living "in the now." His Word says that if we're faithful in a few things, then He will put us in charge of many things. That promise implies a certain amount of waiting—and that there is blessing in patience and virtue in endurance. Thus, if the Lord's people are dependable with their talents and gifts, they can look forward to more in the future—even in today's restless, seize-the-day, grabbing-the-gusto society. With God, all things are imaginable and achievable! —AH

God, give me patience as I wait and help me to live joyfully in all circumstances. Amen.

What's in It for Me?

*"Whoever wants to become great
among you must be your servant."*
MATTHEW 20:26 NIV

Years ago, the comment "You scratch my back,
and I'll scratch yours" was used so often it
became a hackneyed expression. People may not
say it as much as they once did, but the concept
is still well-rooted in society. Unfortunately, the
fruit that comes from such a mindset is not as
tasty and sweet as it was meant to be. Because
of societal conditioning, it's easier to help folks
when there is a mutual understanding that both
parties are expected to benefit from trading
kindnesses. Sounds more contractual than
compassionate, doesn't it?

But what happens when someone steps out of the usual communal rut and goes way out of her way to offer help to a traveler in trouble, with the deed-doer wanting nothing in return? To witness those life moments or to be the actual recipient of such kindness tends to stay in a person's heart and memory forever. That's because people know those "happy surprises," where good deeds are offered without any expectation of reciprocation, are becoming more and more uncommon. Perhaps the best question for daily living is, "God, what can I do for someone You love?" The branches of such a divine appeal would bring forth the best fruit— and the most soul-satisfying harvest. —AH

God, help me to love, serve, and sacrifice without expecting anything in return. Amen.

A Dirty Business

---

*"Now that I, your Lord and Teacher,
have washed your feet, you also should wash
one another's feet. I have set you an example
that you should do as I have done for you."*

JOHN 13:14–15 NIV

Life is a dirty business. And in Bible times it was
even dirtier, because then people were more exposed
to the elements. They didn't have paved roads, and
folks walked a lot—in sandals. So, washing one's
or another's feet was common and necessary. Even
though doing so is no longer necessary, there's still
plenty of significance in this passage regarding a
humbleness of attitude. Yet the concept of *humility*,
almost a foreign word today, makes people squirm.

That's because humility connotes a life of submissive kind-heartedness, an intimate connection with the needs of humanity, and a dying to oneself. Doesn't sound like go-getter advice from a life coach, a plan to get ahead in business, or a way to climb the proverbial ladder of success. How in the world could anyone put on airs or be "cool" when kneeling down to wash the grime off someone else's feet—especially if the person with the grubby, calloused heels has a prideful expression? Perhaps that was Jesus' point exactly. Humility is the road less traveled and yet is the dusty road Christ has asked us to walk. Yes, humility is a dirty business—but a holy one. —AH

God, help me to serve as You served:
selflessly, humbly, and relentlessly. Amen.

The Golden Light

Do nothing out of selfish ambition or vain conceit. Rather, in humility value others above yourselves, not looking to your own interests but each of you to the interests of the others.
PHILIPPIANS 2:3–4 NIV

Moms and dads generally tell their little darlings from birth that they are the golden light of their parents' existence. That they will grow up to be the best of the best. The chosen ones for greatness. True rising stars in whatever field they choose to shine in.

The Bible doesn't say we can't have goals or interests or dreams, and that we aren't to equip ourselves for the future. But the Word does say that we are to consider the interests of others, too, even beyond our own desires. That's a heavy calling and one so contrary to modern thinking that it will take a lifetime to embrace it fully. This new path will take a miraculous transformation of heart and a daily commitment to walk in God's way. It is such a strange dichotomy—such a sacred mystery—to know that the greatest among us will always be the servant to all. —AH

God, even though I deserve nothing,
You shower love and grace upon me.
Help me to do the same for others. Amen.

Starting Small

*Put on then, as God's chosen ones,
holy and beloved, compassionate hearts,
kindness, humility, meekness, and patience.*
Colossians 3:12 esv

Being the kind of servant that Jesus commanded His followers to be may seem like a daunting and nebulous task. Where does one begin? Serving at a soup kitchen might come to mind. Digging a well in the sweltering heat for an impoverished village. Taking orphans and vagabonds into one's home. While these are incredible and worthy tasks, these opportunities may not come up every day. But the chance to serve a stranger, family member, friend, or foe will present itself constantly. Doing things for others can start with the simplest act. Listening and showing genuine concern for their worries and frustrations, sacrificing time for them, speaking truth into their lives, or perhaps responding graciously to insults.

These little deeds may seem unimpressive and inconsequential, but they can have a profound effect on someone's life. Being a servant means considering someone else's needs to be more important than your own. It means cherishing and delighting in people and extending compassion to them as Christ does for us. —HM

God, give me the eyes to see how I can serve others on a daily basis, no matter how small the act may appear. Amen.

Putting Aside the Gavel

"Judge not, that you be not judged."
MATTHEW 7:1 ESV

Often, judgments are made quicker than a lightning strike. The gavel has fallen, and the verdict is pronounced before there has been any attempt at true understanding. The appraiser's accusations can be gleaned from another's outward appearance, attitude, or circumstances. A homeless man. A grumpy sales clerk. A pregnant teenager. Judgment can even extend beyond strangers and affect the way one views close friends or family members, especially ones who keep making poor decisions despite the constant advice and prayer of others.

It's easy to feel elevated above the sorrowful, stubborn soul who refuses to put wisdom into action. The self-righteous occupy the judge's seat with authority and superiority, feeling that she has the greater good on her side. However, this outlook keeps those who have been deemed unworthy at arm's length. The judges believe they have evaluated thoroughly the case of the accused; they have weighed the guilty party's life on a scale and found him or her wanting.

But only God knows the heart and mind of the accused. Only God can wield the gavel. Our job is to love as Christ has loved, with great compassion and wild abandon. Rather than holding humanity at arm's length with an appraising eye, embrace it with ready arms, one soul at a time. —HM

God, instead of allowing judgment to reign in my heart, help me to love with grace. Amen.

The Least of These

"For I was hungry and you gave me food,
I was thirsty and you gave me drink,
I was a stranger and you welcomed me."
MATTHEW 25:35 ESV

Sometimes, those who need help the most are the easiest people to withdraw from or ignore. Caring for those who are suffering or unwanted— the impoverished drug addict or the annoying, offensive coworker who eats lunch alone—is often a troublesome and unwelcome task.

Every day, we are brought into contact with those who are hurting and anxious, their desperation thinly disguised by a vacant smile. It can be tempting for the busy, overburdened woman to overlook a fellow struggling soul, to press on with her day and deal with her own problems, remaining within her comfort zone.

But if she were to pause and offer a hand, whether for someone in need of daily necessities or someone with a discouraged and downcast spirit, she is also reaching out to Jesus through her kind words and provision. In a life full of activity, it can be difficult to remember that the people we pass in the grocery store, at work, or on the street have been handcrafted by God and are as full of conflicting emotions, desires, and disappointments as we are. A selfless act of love will shine the light of Christ on those who need it. —HM

God, give me the strength, patience, and wisdom I need to reach out to others. Amen.

A Half Life

*[God] created us anew in Christ Jesus, so we can
do the good things he planned for us long ago.*
EPHESIANS 2:10 NLT

Christianity isn't just a list of don'ts. Nor is it
merely a charge for the devout to grit their teeth,
abstaining from all activities they are secretly
drawn to. Nor is it to be used as a means to
make the believer feel self-righteous because she
doesn't participate in the deeds of secular society.

Christianity is meant to be a torch, bringing
hope and light to people who are desperate to
have a purpose greater than that of fulfilling
their own desires. A Christian's goal is to seek
out those needing love, assistance, and prayer.
She is to see beyond the painted-on smile of a
neighbor or coworker, to not shy away from the
grief or troubles of others but try to uplift them
and bring them closer to Christ.

Judging the value of a life on the basis of all the things one *hasn't* done bespeaks a hollow, fruitless existence. If a Christian's sole purpose were to refrain from sinning, she would live a strange half-life, sequestered away from society and temptations.

But how can one possibly resist all sinful impulses and also be a humble servant to all humanity? These feats are only attainable through Christ's provision and grace. Only by clinging to Him can we accomplish the impossible. —HM

God, help me to find joy in my duties as a Christian. May my actions glorify You. Amen.

Priceless Gems

*Teach us to number our days that
we may get a heart of wisdom.*
PSALM 90:12 ESV

Time is one of the most precious treasures humans
can possess. It is incredibly valuable because, once
spent, it is irretrievable. Like a vast collection
of priceless gems, time constantly slips through
people's fingers, full of infinite potential and worth
but so often wasted.

For some, the passage of time is frighteningly
clear. They may cling to it, jealous and possessive,
wanting to spend it only on those activities that
bring them gain or comfort. Others might disregard
the value of time completely, allowing it to depart
from them in a steady flow, unnoticed and misused.

But to assume that humans are the masters of
their time on earth is to forget the Creator. Humans

have nothing apart from God, and the time He has granted them is a gift and an opportunity to encounter Him. When His children remember that their time is not their own and recognize God as the genuine possessor, they will want to use it for His glory. Time that was once hoarded or squandered will instead be sacrificed for the good of others through acts of service. Surrendering our time to the Father will help us become more devoted and faithful servants to Him. —HM

God, help me to use my days wisely for Your glory. Thank You for the gift of time. Amen.

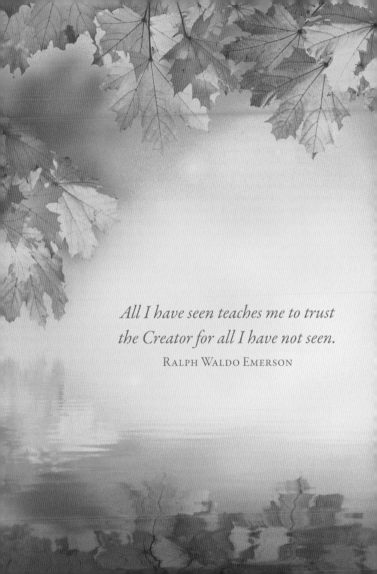

*All I have seen teaches me to trust
the Creator for all I have not seen.*

RALPH WALDO EMERSON

Viewing Life from
Heaven's Porch

Your Birthday into Heaven

However, as it is written: "What no eye has seen, what no ear has heard, and what no human mind has conceived"—the things God has prepared for those who love him.

1 CORINTHIANS 2:9 NIV

If the most brilliant minds in the world had a symposium on heaven, and together they fashioned the most creative and dazzling ideas ever conceived on what heaven could be like, it would not come close to what you will know on that great gasping day of earth's goodbye—and then your birthday into heaven!

The senses will no doubt be awakened with colors, aromas, tastes, textures, and mysteries never experienced before. And the light, oh, the holy light of God. There is no artificial light or natural earthly glow that can come close to the sublimely golden luminosity of the Creator of the universe. Even the most extravagant of human adjectives are inadequate to express all that heaven will hold.

Imagine the most beautiful place on earth where you've vacationed, and yet that spectacular memory cannot come close to the infinite majesty and rapture and wonder in the dwelling place of God. —AH

God, I'm excited to see what You have in store for me! May the hope of my eternal home bring me comfort and confidence. Amen.

Man's Illusion of Light

There will be no more night. They will not
need the light of a lamp or the light of the sun,
for the Lord God will give them light.
And they will reign for ever and ever.
Revelation 22:5 niv

The moment the first earthly couple touched
and tasted that forbidden fruit in the Garden of
Eden, men and women have been running into
the shadows, the misty gloom of night, hiding
from the holy beacon of God's light. Since that
fallen moment, that disobedient act, people have
been pretending all is well, but man's illusion of
light has failed—it is merely a spiritual conjuring
trick of the enemy. Thank God He sent His
Son to rescue humankind from that distorted
existence.

When you accept Christ for what He is—King of Kings and Lord of Lords—the hiding can cease, and the light of Christ can shine through your smile, your deeds, your life. And then when that appointed hour arrives that all humans must face, imagine opening your eyes to a place where there is no more night, no more dark, trembling places of gloom—for all eternity. Where light is celebrated, embraced, and reflected. Imagine heaven. . . . —AH

God, don't allow me to be fooled by the enemy's pale and sickly imitation of Your light. Help me to cling to what is pure and holy. Amen.

Summits of Greatness

But our citizenship is in heaven. And we eagerly await a Savior from there, the Lord Jesus Christ, who, by the power that enables him to bring everything under his control, will transform our lowly bodies so that they will be like his glorious body.
PHILIPPIANS 3:20–21 NIV

Humans were meant to be so much more than they are. Adam and Eve must surely have had brilliant minds, beautiful and strong physiques, and gorgeous spirits that took invention and imagination to heights modern man can only dream of.

People were made for summits of greatness, not slums of iniquity. They waste their time on gossip, grumbling, fretting, and malicious deeds. These are precious moments that could have been spent in creative thought, loving and being loved, and noble endeavors. People could choose to sprinkle goodwill on others, like Scrooge on Christmas morning. Men and women could bless the day rather than curse the air with destructive speech.

Ask God to let you see how He sees people, how He loves them. Don't wait until you go to heaven to begin your closer walk with the Lord. Ask the Holy Spirit to begin His sanctification in you now, that you may live with victory—with heaven in your heart every day until you step from this life and into the next. —AH

---

*God, help me to become all
You created me to be. Amen.*

The Promise of Heaven

" 'He will wipe every tear from their eyes. There will be no more death' or mourning or crying or pain, for the old order of things has passed away."
<small>REVELATION 21:4 NIV</small>

When a child falls and hurts himself, his parents panic. Moms and dads arrive armed with Band-Aids, soothing words, tissues, and a hug, but God comes armed with so much more—the promise to wipe away all tears forever, the promise of heaven for those who choose to follow Him.

Think of it. To never need a hospital or a doctor again. To never lose a spouse from death or watch families be torn apart by divorce. To never know the shame of sin or the tears of disappointment, to depart forever from the continual sting of an errant planet rocked with crime, pain, and violence. No more wars or disease or disasters.

The knowledge of heaven should make us rejoice and shout the news. It should change the way we put our head down on the pillow and face the night, how we wake up in the morning, and how we live every minute we have breath in our lungs. Heaven changes everything! —AH

God, may my faith in Your grace and my anticipation of heaven radically transform my life. Make me fearless, joyful, and loving. Amen.

The Fingerprint of the Creator

But thanks be to God! He gives us the
victory through our Lord Jesus Christ.
1 CORINTHIANS 15:57 NIV

Humans yearn to make order and beauty out of
chaos. Even when people do their gardening, they
toil and sweat for months, trying to turn a mere
pile of dirt and weeds into a tiny corner of paradise.
Man has a deep need to see positive transformation
in all aspects of life, from the seeds of the earth to
the soul. That desire is like a holy fingerprint left
behind by the Creator on all of mankind—and it
is a desire that could never be washed away, even
from the Fall. That imprint is there on every human
heart, and it drives people to want understanding
over confusion. They want victory over defeat. They
want to see what is broken restored.

But man can never make things right again—only God can. Jesus Christ brings the ultimate order and beauty out of the chaos of man's soul. He fulfills the yearning that no person can fulfill on her own. And someday those who love the Lord will no longer have to work with this hardened earth—heaven will no longer be a place to hope for but a place of residence. —AH

God, thank You for the hope I have in You. Help me to remember that only You can fulfill, restore, and create true order. Amen.

A Mere Glimpse

O LORD, how manifold are your works!
In wisdom have you made them all;
the earth is full of your creatures.
PSALM 104:24 ESV

One of the clearest windows into heaven is
through the brilliance and beauty of nature. In
today's air-conditioned, insulated, windowless
world, it can be easy to become shut off from
God's creation. The outdoors merely becomes
a place to walk through when going from one
building to another. But nature can still be
encountered on the commute to work, on a
porch swing, or through an open window. God's
incredible attention to detail can be found in
the intricate patterns of a butterfly's wing. His
majesty can be seen in the white marble of the
clouds.

Humans can gain insight into their Creator by studying and appreciating His creation. Would God have made a sloth or a duckbill platypus if He didn't have a sense of humor? Would He have made a kitten's fur so soft if He didn't have tenderness? And would He have created the sweet aroma of a gardenia or the crisp freshness of a fall day if He didn't want humans to experience pleasure? If earth is only a mere glimpse into heaven, then what joys and incredible sights await Christians in eternity! — HM

God, thank You for the beauty of creation. Help me to see it with new eyes every day. Amen.

Nesting in the Clouds

*"For where your treasure is,
there your heart will be also."*
MATTHEW 6:21 ESV

Women are natural nesters. It's tempting for them
to want to bed down and be comfortable in the
world they've been planted in. To all outward and
secular perspectives, this life is the entire show, and
death is the grand finale. If that were the truth, it
would make sense to be tethered to one's only home
and to commit to its values and customs. Society
and culture have a tendency to persuade people that
the greatest end is to attain success in a career and
to have a healthy, loving family in a nice home,
with time and money to travel after retirement.+

While these are beautiful and good things, this is not the ultimate end for Christians. Their purpose is so much larger than just procuring a relatively enjoyable and relaxing existence. These things will tarnish with age, but a life spent seeking God and loving others will echo on through eternity. What does your heart gravitate toward? What is your greatest treasure? The answers to these questions will determine the entire focus and ambition of your life. —HM

God, I want You to be at the center of my existence and the most valuable treasure in my life. Amen.

The Seeds of Eternity

Yet God has made everything beautiful for its own time. He has planted eternity in the human heart, but even so, people cannot see the whole scope of God's work from beginning to end.
ECCLESIASTES 3:11 NLT

Fathoming the infinite is almost impossible for the human mind. All man-made stories and songs have a beginning and an end. Oceans have boundaries, and mountains have peaks. Everything has a shelf life. Surrounded by such temporal and finite things, how can the human mind visualize something existing for all eternity? When one tries to break the barriers of time by stretching her imagination out into the unknown, trying to envision an existence unbroken by death, she might find herself overwhelmed by the incredible length of it.

Yet God has planted eternity in the human heart. There are latent seeds buried deep in the soil of our souls, waiting to sprout. The human soul has no end; it will extend forever. Our earthly minds may not be able to grasp the scope of it yet, but on the day when those who have accepted Jesus reach the end of this life, their eyes will be opened, and understanding will be granted. —HM

God, thank You for my eternal home, even if I can't comprehend it now. Help me not to forget it in the distractions of this life. Amen.

Legacy of Love

The aim of our charge is love that issues from a pure heart and a good conscience and a sincere faith.
1 TIMOTHY 1:5 ESV

Leaving behind a legacy is an important and deep-seated need in many people. They want to make an imprint that will keep them alive in the memories of others, and many desire to create a permanent change in the world for the better. Often, they want to be remembered for their intelligence, creativity, athleticism, or wisdom. They want to be immortalized by writing a book, winning a game, or making a new discovery.

However, the occasion that we believe to be our finest hour or the achievement that we hold in highest esteem may not be the moment or accomplishment that is most celebrated and praised in heaven. While working diligently in a career is incredibly necessary and admirable, Christians shouldn't discount the lasting impact of love. Showing kindness when it's undeserved, accepting the awkward and lonely, and extending compassion to the hurting might seem like small and insignificant acts on the surface, but they will not be overlooked by God or forgotten in eternity.

Although it's tempting to bend every effort to obtaining recognition and approval on earth, remember that the greatest legacy is to love others in Christ's name. —HM

God, may my legacy be that I made much of You instead of myself. Amen.

Unseen Enemies

Be sober-minded; be watchful. Your adversary
the devil prowls around like a roaring lion,
seeking someone to devour.
1 PETER 5:8 ESV

Often, people believe their worst enemies are
those they can see, hear, or feel. The scariest foes
seem to be the things that threaten their bodies,
reputations, pride, or livelihood. An illness, loss
of a job, heartbreak, or a hateful neighbor.

But there are much greater enemies lurking
beyond human sight. Even some Christians
discount or forget about the existence of
demonic forces and their endless attempts to
beckon and persuade humans into sin. While on
earth, people are forever caught in the crosshairs
of the devil and his legion. He is cunning in
his deceit and persistent in his attacks. And
his highest aim is infinitely worse than causing

temporary harm. Through false promises and lies, Satan coaxes souls into the darkness to be forever separated from God. There is no end more disastrous than this.

However, as Christians we have nothing to fear. By accepting Christ, we have made a home in heaven. Nevertheless, we must remain aware of Satan's pervasive influences, lest he creep in through an unwatched door. We can be vigilant by equipping ourselves with knowledge of the Word and by maintaining a strong bond with our Creator. —HM

God, help me to remember who my true enemies are, and instruct me in how to resist them. Amen.

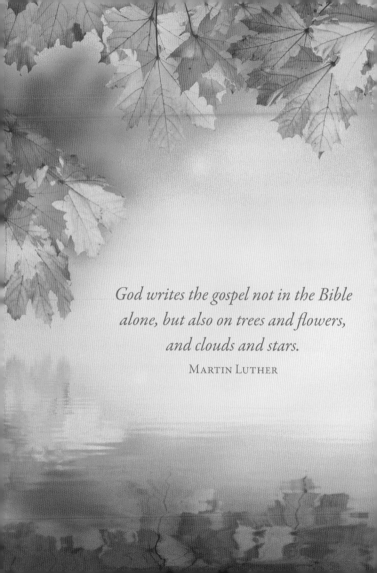

*God writes the gospel not in the Bible
alone, but also on trees and flowers,
and clouds and stars.*

MARTIN LUTHER

Reflecting the Beauty of Mercy

Walking in the Savior's Footsteps

"Blessed are the merciful."
MATTHEW 5:7 NIV

When a person is on the receiving end of a great act of mercy, it can be life-changing. Victor Hugo's masterpiece *Les Misérables* begins with this epic theme. The story opens with a thief being the recipient of unmerited mercy, and that amazing deed changes the character's life in a beautiful way. That powerful beginning scene also reflects the kind of redeeming love that Christ offers through His death and resurrection.

The Almighty is not only merciful, but He expects His beloved creatures to cultivate the same holy quality toward others, even though mercy isn't easy to offer to people, especially those who are continually bent on sinful behavior. It doesn't mean that people shouldn't receive justice if what they've done is illegal, but justice and mercy can go hand in hand—and forgiveness is an act of mercy.

Jesus says, "Blessed are the merciful." So, offer compassion with a generous and genuine spirit, and in those moments, always remember, you will be walking in the Savior's footsteps. —AH

God, give me the strength to forgive those who have wronged me. I want to be an imitator of You. Amen.

The Whole Spa Experience

"Come to me, all you who are weary and burdened, and I will give you rest. Take my yoke upon you and learn from me, for I am gentle and humble in heart, and you will find rest for your souls. For my yoke is easy and my burden is light."

MATTHEW 11:28–30 NIV

Women love the whole spa experience—facials, pedicures, massages. In fact, those kinds of establishments seem to be flourishing. Why is that? Most likely, people are looking for ways to unwind from the exhausting realities of their weekly grind. Perhaps they have a job that doesn't satisfy, friends who don't act very friendly, a marriage that is struggling to keep afloat, bills that keep piling up, children who are disobedient, and a host of other trials that keep people in a constant state of turmoil.

Jesus' promise in Matthew is a little like a spa experience, only for the soul. "Come to me, all you who are weary and burdened, and I will give you rest." That sounds like something every person is in great need of—right now—this very minute. If you take God up on His offer, it will be the one "yes" you will never regret, either in this life, or in the one to come. —AH

God, help me to relax in Your promises and comforts. Thank You for taking away my every burden, big and small. Amen.

Not Just for a Day or a Season

For the LORD is good and his love endures forever;
his faithfulness continues through all generations.
PSALM 100:5 NIV

When life is smoothing along well, it's not all
that difficult to show compassion toward others.
But when things get tough or messy, an uncaring
spirit can rise to the surface all too quickly.
Keeping a calloused attitude at bay while
surrounded by such a hard-hearted world isn't
easy, but with a commitment to a daily devotion
time and prayer, it's doable. Also, it's important
to remember the times when people showed
you tender mercy—the times when it wasn't
deserved but deeply appreciated—and then,
hopefully, granting mercy to others will come
more easily.

God grants His children these same gentle mercies, again and again and again—to the point where His children might look up and wonder why. But it's in the Lord's nature to do so. Not only is He a God of justice, but He also has great forbearance, and according to Psalms, His mercy endures not just for a day or a season, but His mercy endures forever. —AH

God, thank You for granting me undeserved mercy. Give me the compassion and strength to extend it to others. Amen.

A Cup of Mercy

Yet the LORD longs to be gracious to you; therefore he will rise up to show you compassion. For the LORD is a God of justice. Blessed are all who wait for him!
ISAIAH 30:18 NIV

The Lord longs to be gracious to everyone, so we should rise up every morning with the same yearning in our spirits. There are a thousand ways to show compassion to others. One especially poignant way is to not pronounce judgment on people. Humans are notoriously bad at it. They generally condemn the sinner right along with the transgression. And even when there's no sin involved, people will scrutinize another person's clothing, weight, speech, haircut, demeanor, etc., and become that person's judge and jury in less than five minutes.

But how many times have your conclusions been wrong? Appearances can be deceptive. No one knows the whole story about another person. Only God knows the infinitesimal details of another, the inner travails, the history—all of it. That's one of the reasons Jesus said to take the beam out of your own eye so you could see clearly to remove the speck of sawdust from your sister's eye.

So, the next time there's an urge to anoint someone with judgment, offer her a cup of mercy instead. —AH

God, give me a merciful and accepting spirit.
I have no right to judge. Amen.

Blessed in the Act of Giving

It is a sin to despise one's neighbor,
but blessed is the one who is kind to the needy.
PROVERBS 14:21 NIV

People who are poor tend to be neglected by society. Even the homeless on the streets become part of the world's "invisibles." But God sees the needy, and He wouldn't want them to be passed over. To simply ignore those who suffer with the pain and humiliation of poverty is perhaps just another form of scorn.

It's natural to think that the money in one's own bank account is well deserved from hard work, but the truth is—everything on this earth belongs to God. Whatever is in your storehouse comes from His hand and His mercy, and just as you teach your children to share, God enjoys seeing His children share their blessings. Those who watch out for the needy are considered precious in God's eyes. They are blessed in the act of giving. How wonderful it is to see a new light of hope in someone's eyes when you've given her a helping hand. When you've reached out to her, knowing you have support and even praise from God Himself. —AH

God, soften my heart toward the poor.
Give me the opportunity and the courage
to help someone in need today. Amen.

Broken Bonds

*For freedom Christ has set us free; stand firm
therefore, and do not submit again to a yoke of slavery.*
GALATIANS 5:1 ESV

A shameful sin can stick closer than a shadow.
It stalks quietly, silent but ever present. It casts
darkness and makes for an unwelcome, phantom
companion. It is common for people's bad decisions
and mistakes to lurk in the back of their minds,
impossible to shake, tainting any future joy with its
memory and chipping away at their peace.

Even the most devout Christians suffer from
this affliction. Although they have accepted Jesus'
grace, they have allowed it to cover only their
smaller, more "excusable" sins. The monstrous
errors, the ones that get shoved into a dark corner,
seem too ghastly to be forgiven. It doesn't seem

possible that these iniquities could be cast aside by a holy God and forgotten forever.

The good news is that Christ's grace blankets every sin, covering the unintentional and unknown mistakes as well as the sins that make the perpetrator cringe with regret and shame. He has broken your bonds and released you from the slavery of sin. You have the freedom to pursue a life unburdened by the past, allowing you to live out the present to its fullest. —HM

God, help me to trust in the power of Your grace. Thank You for Your sacrifice. Amen.

Joyful Abandon

"Truly, I say to you, unless you turn and become like children, you will never enter the kingdom of heaven."
MATTHEW 18:3 ESV

Imagine a child on Christmas morning. Her delight at the bright, colorful packages under the tree and the promise of hours of enjoyment hidden beneath the wrapping. Most likely, the little girl has done nothing to deserve the gifts. Yet she accepts them all without question and with great joy and gratitude. Unfortunately, people may find Christ's grace a little harder to accept than a Christmas present. The concept of complete forgiveness for all their sins can be a difficult thing to grasp. And even harder to fathom is the fact that His grace is a free gift—it can't possibly be earned by their own merit.

When Jesus' disciples asked Him who would be the greatest in the kingdom of heaven, He responded by calling a small child to Him and telling them that if they became humble like a little child, they would be the greatest in heaven. Contrary to the world's definition of greatness, Jesus was asking them to become lowly and meek, with a deep realization of their inability to achieve forgiveness through any effort of their own. Just as a child will throw herself at the foot of the Christmas tree to tear open her gifts, so should we approach Christ's grace with joyful abandon. —HM

God, thank You for the free gift of grace.
Help me to accept it without inhibitions or fear.
Amen.

The Other Son

"Just so, I tell you, there is joy before the angels of God over one sinner who repents."
LUKE 15:10 ESV

Sometimes, all the trappings of the Christian lifestyle—memorizing scripture, tithing faithfully, praying for others, attending services, mission trips, fundraisers, and Bible studies—can be used as a desperate attempt to earn the favor of God. For the weary Christian caught in this charade, the joy and pleasure will eventually begin to fade from these activities, making church a chore and God a distant and untouchable being.

So when a lost soul finds grace and enters the church, all ablaze with a newfound fervor for God, the overworked Christians might feel neglected, envious, or even angry. Like the prodigal son's older brother—the one who remained loyal to his father and toiled in the fields—they may wonder why their hard work goes uncelebrated.

And like little children, they impatiently hold out their hands for the prize they believe they have earned through obedience, when in fact the rewards have already been laid at their feet, ready to be taken and enjoyed. It's not possible to obtain any more of God's love through our own works. By believing in Jesus, we are given all we need. As the father says to his oldest son in the prodigal's parable: "All that is mine is yours" (Luke 15:31 ESV). —HM

God, I'm thankful that Your love for me is not based on my works. Amen.

Pardoning Debts

"And should not you have had mercy on your fellow servant, as I had mercy on you?"
MATTHEW 18: 33 ESV

To remember a wrong is to feel a certain sense of invulnerability and security, as if by never letting go, the victim can prevent that harm from ever happening to her again. In comparison, forgiveness and mercy seem weak. Viewing the situation through the eyes of justice alone, the offender should be punished and cast aside, deserving neither a clean slate nor an act of love.

In one of Jesus' parables, a king discovers that a servant owes him an enormous debt, too large to pay off in any lifetime. Yet, because of his great kindness, the king decides to forgive the servant. Later, the forgiven man finds a fellow servant who owes him money, and—although it's a miniscule fraction of what the forgiven man owed the king—he begins to strangle the other man, demanding repayment. When the king hears about his servant's mercilessness, even after being pardoned, the king is angry and hands him over to the jailer.

Like the first servant, we have been forgiven a debt that has accumulated to a size beyond our comprehension. Yet we have only to ask and we are forgiven. Christ's grace is shocking in its magnitude and eagerness. And because of the forgiveness extended to us through Christ, so should we forgive the debts of others. —HM

---

*God, give me the strength
to pardon all. Amen.*

Redeemed, how I love to proclaim it!... His child, and forever, I am.

FANNY CROSBY

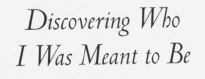

Discovering Who
I Was Meant to Be

Grocery Store Fandango

*"Do to others as you would
have them do to you."*
LUKE 6:31 NIV

Being wedged in a long, snail-paced line at the
grocery checkout puts everyone on edge. It's
easy to start huffing and puffing, rolling one's
eyes, and generally trying to make the person
behind the counter wish she'd called in sick or
never even applied for the job! On a better day
that same check-out person might tell bits of her
story. She might say that she has to work two
jobs since her husband got laid off. She might
reveal how badly her feet ache. Or that she's still
recovering from a cold.

It's hard to ignore or get feisty with strangers when their lives are spread out for all to see. When you know a bit of their personal story. After all, now the person is seen as someone who is just like you—a fellow sojourner, not an employee or worse, a mere cog in the wheel of commerce. The whole world can be changed, one smile at a time, and sometimes it starts with beaming one to the lady with aching feet standing behind the counter. —AH

God, help me to reflect Your light wherever I go. Open my eyes to people's needs and frustrations, and allow me to be a soothing balm in their lives. Amen.

Going a New Way

"Watch and pray so that you will not fall into temptation. The spirit is willing, but the flesh is weak."
MATTHEW 26:41 NIV

Temptations abound in this life. They come in every shape and size. And some come tailor-made by the enemy to fit your very weaknesses. So how can people be who they were meant to be if they are constantly being bombarded with distractions and enticements to become something far less than God's true potential for them?

Jesus tells us that humans may be willing to do what is right, but their flesh is not always so happy to oblige. That statement becomes obvious at mealtime when one is on a diet. A person might have the knowledge of how to lose weight. She might be determined to follow through with her diet plan. But come mealtime, the appetite, which is controlled by the flesh, may very well win in spite of the knowledge and will to change.

The Lord knows this weakness in humanity all too well, which is why Jesus said, "Watch and pray so you won't fall into temptation." Prayer always seems like the simple answer. Too simple, right? And yet it is the very power tool Jesus used against Satan when tempted in the desert. It is still the best power tool today. Use it liberally. —AH

God, You have given me the power to resist temptation. Help me to come to You in moments of weakness. Amen.

The Long Run Ahead

Consider it pure joy, my brothers and sisters,
whenever you face trials of many kinds,
because you know that the testing of your
faith produces perseverance.
JAMES 1:2–3 NIV

No one likes hardships. They're as much fun as a sledgehammer on a sore toe. But God tells His children that they should consider trials joy—pure joy. That comment feels foreign to most folks, but God offers an encouraging aspect to this curious declaration: With trials comes perseverance. Various Bible translations also use the words *patience*, *steadfastness*, *endurance*, and *strength*. Just as a person who's lived a couch-potato lifestyle cannot expect to run a marathon or even trot across the parking lot without getting winded, Christians who experience little adversity cannot expect to gain enough strength for the long run ahead. And life—even the Christian life—is indeed a long and sometimes uphill race.

Helen Keller said, "Character cannot be developed in ease and quiet. Only through experience of trial and suffering can the soul be strengthened, ambition inspired, and success achieved." The natural tendency is to turn away from that truth because of its harshness, and yet it must be embraced for a healthy and whole Christian life. Here lies paradox as well as peace.
—AH

God, help me to learn and improve from trials and sorrows. May they help me become who You want me to be. Amen.

A Bad 'Tude

Therefore, if anyone is in Christ, the new creation has come: The old has gone, the new is here!
2 CORINTHIANS 5:17 NIV

How do you want to be remembered? At your funeral, when the minister says, "She was a wonderfully kind person whom everyone loved," will people be rolling their eyes? Some folks, even Christians, seem to have been born with a bad 'tude, and they never seem to get over it. Even when lovely things happen to them, they can't help but find the ugly-duckling angle on the beautiful-swan moment. Sound familiar?

If that person is you, here's how you can banish that 'tude. First, seek out some honest feedback from a trusted friend or two who knows how to sandwich the truth in love. Second, accept the truth if it's valid, even though it might be painful.

Third, give God an open season on your heart to shoot down any and all ugly 'tudes. Finally, let the Holy Spirit guide you so that you can become a new creation. When the old has gone and the new is here, you will emerge like a butterfly from a cocoon—beautiful and miraculous and with wings ready to fly! —AH

God, help me to shrug off old habits and to embrace a lifestyle and attitude that is pleasing to You and others. Amen.

The Perfect Fit

*"See that you fulfill the ministry
that you have received in the Lord."*
Colossians 4:17 esv

For some people, finding a good career or
pursuit can be as difficult and frustrating as
trying to find the perfect shoes in a store where
nothing seems to fit. At first glance, a pair may
look like the right size and style, but after trying
them on, the shoes pinch or make blisters.

Passionate and driven women may attempt
to wear many different pairs of shoes before they
find the right fit. They might cram their tired
feet into narrow heels, hoping to find fulfillment
in business when they are naturally inclined to
music, writing, or teaching. Desperately trying
to fill roles they feel are meant for them, these
well-intentioned women clomp around in

uncomfortable shoes, all the while feeling inadequate or dissatisfied with their work.

But God did not mean for His children to slouch or wince through life, feeling defeated in all their endeavors. He has gifted everyone uniquely, and He will guide us to our special niche if we maintain an open mind and a receptive heart. The right calling may be totally different from what we'd imagined, but through it we can best use our God-given abilities for His glory. —HM

God, help me to pursue the work that You have set aside for me and to excel in it exalting You and not myself. Amen.

House of Cards

I count everything as loss because of the surpassing worth of knowing Christ Jesus my Lord.
PHILIPPIANS 3:8 ESV

Musician, homemaker, businesswoman, activist. Occupations and pursuits are sometimes so all-consuming that it can be easy for the ambitious woman to begin to base her identity in her employment. On the surface, it's a tantalizing idea to be known as a talented artist or a charitable person. It gives her a sense of pride to have fabricated a name for herself.

Unfortunately, her sense of self-worth might have a tendency to become tightly bound to her abilities and achievements. And when she inevitably experiences frustration or failure in her efforts, her identity will tumble like a house of cards. The woman whose value is tied up in her accomplishments will feel crushed and insignificant because the one thing that had broadcasted her worth has proved unsound and temporal.

The only foolproof way to recognize the depth of one's value is to realize that it's founded in Christ. His love for the ambitious woman remains the same despite her inabilities and insufficiencies. He is constant and unchanging, steadfast and eternal. If she remembers that her identity is based on deep love and unfailing mercy, it will not be subject to the fluctuations of life's disappointments. The strongest and surest identity is one that relies on Christ's daily grace. —HM

God, help me to remember that I am worth more than anything I could possibly accomplish. You define my value. Amen.

From Dwelling to Delight

He led me to a place of safety;
he rescued me because he delights in me.
2 SAMUEL 22:20 NLT

For some women, dwelling on their imperfections and flaws can be a daily occupation. Merciless mirrors reveal ill-fitting clothes or untamable hair. Throughout the day, all their efforts seem to fall short; all their best qualities seem insufficient. To the dispirited woman, her own personality quirks begin to seem like defects, and the accomplishments that had once brought her pride now seem like ant hills to someone else's mountains.

Sometimes, her kindness might fail to conquer her irritation, envy may smolder in her heart, and selfish thoughts war within. On these days, feeling unlovable and downtrodden, there seems to be such a wide expanse between the person she is and the person she wants to be.

Yet despite all her faults and mistakes, God delights in her, even on her worst day. Perched on the edge of the clouds and inclining His ear to hear her call, He is prepared and waiting to rescue her at any time. The Creator finds great pleasure and joy in His creation. Even when we feel like a failure or a nuisance, He loves us unconditionally. All we have to do is accept it.

—HM

God, how incredible is Your constant delight in me. Help me not to dwell on my inadequacies but to turn to You for encouragement and fulfillment. Amen.

Misguided Magnifying Glass

But far be it from me to boast except
in the cross of our Lord Jesus Christ.
GALATIANS 6:14 ESV

For some people, craving praise and awe from
others can become an insatiable, unhealthy appetite.
Their life becomes propelled by future hopes of
the limelight, daydreaming about it and devouring
it if it comes their way. Receiving recognition or
approval can become almost as important as the
achievement or skill itself; without the admiration
of others, their work seems invalidated and
lackluster.

There is a certain heartsickness that comes from
this need for approval. The shallow provision the
limelight offers is like a food that never permanently
satisfies but instead creates a gnawing, ever-growing

hunger within the soul. It becomes an addiction, the desire for commendation and greatness. To be forgotten or fade into insignificance is their greatest fear. But glory never lasts for long; the flighty masses are soon diverted by someone else's success.

The need to exalt, glorify, and worship is God-given. But humanity has twisted the magnifying glass toward itself and others, when it should be focused on the heavens, applauding the One who is worthy of all praise: the creator of all things and the giver of all gifts. If there is to be any boasting, let it be of what can be accomplished with Christ at our side. —HM

God, help me to live not for the approval of others but for You alone. Amen.

Boundless Perfection

To all perfection I see a limit;
but your commands are boundless.
PSALM 119:96 NIV

For a perfectionist, the house can always be neater, a painting can always be better, or a diet can always be healthier. There is always striving but never satisfaction because her expectations are unreachable. When achievements do come her way, she deems them unworthy, and they go uncelebrated and unacknowledged. She sniffs out the flaws in her work like a bloodhound on the scent.

If she does reach some semblance of perfection, she then has the impossible task of maintaining it. The effort is exhausting; attempting flawlessness on one's own steam drains the joy, wonder, and freedom out of life.

All that remains is the steady grit and grind of daily exertion and a growing unease in the spirit, waiting for the inevitable visit of failure.

Despite the perfectionist's best efforts, she is limited by a fallen world and her own human nature. Circumstances will impede her, evil forces may burden her, and her weaknesses might cripple her. This is the lot for inhabitants of an imperfect world. The only flawless being we will ever encounter is God. His perfection is something that we can rely on and embrace. Instead of trying to carve out an immaculate existence through our own merit, let us instead glory in the purity and strength of Christ. —HM

God, You are perfect and holy.
Thank You for Your steadfastness. Amen.

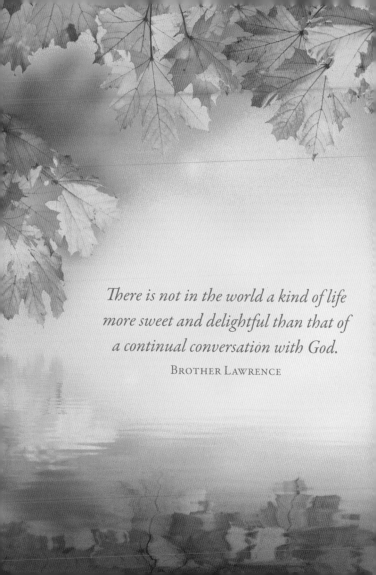

There is not in the world a kind of life more sweet and delightful than that of a continual conversation with God.

BROTHER LAWRENCE

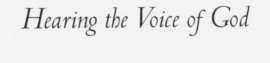

Hearing the Voice of God

The Way of Fools

The way of fools seems right to them,
but the wise listen to advice.
PROVERBS 12:15 NIV

Hearing God through pastors, family, and friends does happen, and the guidance can be quite helpful. But what if the advice turns out to be false? Or what happens when a person becomes too dependent on spiritual direction from others? Is there a time when even trusted friends and relatives overstep their bounds and become a stumbling block to Christian growth by giving too much advice, or perhaps even ungodly advice? The answer is yes!

There are several weights and measures that might be helpful to keep yourself safe from overzealous or despotic mentors. You could ask yourself questions like, "Does this counsel run contrary to anything in the Bible? Are these people trustworthy, and have they proven themselves in the past to be Christlike? Have I created a situation where I'm leaning more on people than prayer?" And then pray about the advice, asking for discernment, and for peace if the guidance should be followed or a lack of peace if the guidance shouldn't.

Even if the advice doesn't lead you to the outcome you'd hoped for, the Lord can redeem all things. Save and rescue is one of God's specialties, and He would be happy for you to make full use of it. —AH

God, give me wisdom in who to pick as my advisors and in what advice to follow. You are the ultimate counselor. Amen.

More Potent Than a Shout

After the earthquake came a fire,
but the LORD was not in the fire.
And after the fire came a gentle whisper.
1 KINGS 19:12 NIV

People might hear from God in a number of unique ways, such as daily events, visions, dreams, and angels. He is the all-powerful God of the universe, and He can reveal Himself to mankind and accomplish His purposes in any way He chooses. One of the more common ways to hear God is through that still, small voice.

The book of 1 Kings tells us that God spoke to the prophet Elijah, not in a thundering earthquake or a blazing inferno, but with a gentle voice.

Sometimes a whisper can be more potent than a shout. And God will speak to you in that same small voice, but your listening is vital. In this modern society—with a thousand noisy distractions and activities—it's easy to miss out on hearing God.

What will it take to slow down? Perhaps realizing that it's more important to fellowship with the One who made you, the One who loves you best, than it is to take ballroom dancing or check out Facebook. —AH

God, life is full of opportunities to stop and focus on Your voice. Don't ever allow my spirit to be in such a flutter that it can't be quiet and listen. Amen.

Through His Living Word

*All Scripture is God-breathed and is useful for
teaching, rebuking, correcting and training in
righteousness, so that the servant of God may be
thoroughly equipped for every good work.*
2 Timothy 3:16–17 niv

No book on earth is like the Bible. The Scriptures
are God-breathed and living, meaning that the
Holy Spirit can use the passages to speak to
everyone who reads them.

The Bible can be life-changing for anyone
who reads it with an open heart. It can be comforting at times, but at other times, uncomfortable. To be rebuked for behavior that one
knows is sinful does not make one sleep well at
night. Nor should it. God's Word will help you
put your spiritual life in order. One could say
that it is a divine compass for the soul. Let it be
your guide by reading it daily and living it well.

As a servant of God, you'll also discover that the Word will equip you for every good work.

Along with the Bible being a sort of GPS, it also offers a history of salvation. And even though it's a book containing many heartbreaking stories, it has a happy conclusion. God wins in the end, and if you choose to follow Him, the Word will lead you right to the open gates of heaven. —AH

God, thank You for providing me with Your Word. Help me to gain a better understanding of Your character by reading it regularly. Amen.

Willing to Bring You Home

"My sheep listen to my voice;
I know them, and they follow me."
JOHN 10:27 NIV

Sheep really do need a shepherd. Left to their own devices, they would bumble around, get lost, fall off cliffs, get entangled in brambles, or be eaten by wolves. Sounds a bit like humans.

Jesus, the Good Shepherd, is the only one who can lead people with genuine compassion and true authority. Without Him, the sheep-people will bumble around and fall off some of life's cliffs, such as abusive relationships, various addictions, illegal activities, or sexual immorality.

Jesus says that His sheep listen to His voice, and they do follow. As long as people stay close to Christ, all should go well, but as soon as they stubbornly take off on their own, there's going to be trouble. Out in the world, they will be vulnerable to the attacks of the enemy, temptations, and their own foolishness.

If you've ever gotten lost while hiking, you know how frightening that can be, and how much comfort sweeps over you when a familiar landmark comes into view. Feeling lost? Think of Jesus and His comforting staff, gathering His flock together after it has wandered off in the wilderness. Remember that He is always willing to bring you back into the fold—to bring you home. —AH

God, help me to know Your voice and to follow it,
even when the urge to wander overcomes me.
I'm lost without You. Amen.

Our True Home

"Remain in me, and I will remain in you.
For a branch cannot produce fruit if it is
severed from the vine, and you cannot be
fruitful unless you remain in me."
JOHN 15:4 NLT

Women, no matter their occupation, are
generally multitaskers. Days begin with a to-
do list. Even before their morning coffee, their
minds are buzzing with chores and errands that
need to be accomplished by the day's end. If
there is a morning quiet time with God, it might
be interrupted by a child's chatter, a ringing
phone, or a hungry pet. However, this is life.
Groceries must be bought, bills paid, children
cared for. Where can someone find a silent spot
to rest her mind and spirit in this fast-paced,
beeping, whirling world?

Jesus told His listeners to remain and rest in Him. This means to abide or to dwell in Him as if He were a home. It's easy to feel the need to shoulder one's pack of worries and duties in the morning, believing that God's presence and assurances can be felt only on relaxing days when the kids are gone and the house is clean. But Christians who put all their hope in Him and trust Him with their plans can find rest and peace in the quiet nook created by the almighty architect—God. —HM

---

*God, help me to place my
hope in You hourly. Amen.*

The Quiet Tracker

The heart of man plans his way,
but the LORD establishes his steps.
PROVERBS 16:9 ESV

Running from the will of God is a tiresome, frightening task. He is always in the back of one's mind, and He pursues stealthily and steadfastly like a quiet tracker through shadowy terrain, never shaken off the trail.

Everyone reaches crossroads in their lives or, perhaps more realistically, encounters the option of many different paths, some crooked, some steep, and some straight. At times, people get stuck at the mouth of this terrifying web of possibilities, paralyzed by the fear of change or the impact of a wrong decision. And sometimes, in the deepest chamber of their spirit, hidden behind doors of self-denial and fear, they feel God nudge them toward a particular path that may not look—to the short-sighted human eye—altogether friendly. God's chosen path might appear lonesome and treacherous, but they have not seen the full length of it. They don't know the unique provision it could offer or the beautiful scenes they may see.

If they give in to God's urging and follow His path, whether the decision includes pursuing a new career, moving to another location, or adopting a different lifestyle, He will uphold them in their journey, create within them a stronger character, and give them the life they were meant to live. —HM

God, thank You for being patient with me even when I'm afraid. I give my life to You. Amen.

More Than a Mirage

*Rejoice in our confident hope. Be patient
in trouble, and keep on praying.*
ROMANS 12:12 NLT

Praying can sometimes feel like a lonely, fruitless
undertaking. On these days, heartfelt requests
and praises seem to hit a wall and bounce back,
sounding empty and futile in the echo. The
disconnected Christian may feel all alone in
her head, and it might seem as though the only
audience to her pleadings are her clasped hands.

This distance between God and the
dispirited Christian can come during any season,
whether it is one of turmoil, prosperity, or
listlessness. To her, even the Bible may seem dry
and irrelevant, fellowship with others shallow,
and church services stiff and unhelpful. She
might have the sense that she is stumbling across
a great desert, lost and thirsty, distracted by

the shimmering mirages that falsely promise fulfillment, comfort, or hope. Although these may provide temporal confidence and euphoria, they are often short-lived.

The only oasis in the midst of a spiritual desert is the reassurance of Christ's resurrection and God's steadfast character. Through the shifting sands of life, the hazy deception of mirages, and the merciless heat of the sun, He remains all powerful, ever present, and is passionately in love with you. Continue to seek Him in everything, whether in trials, blessings, or the mundane. —HM

God, help me not to lose heart when I stagger through the desert. I have cause to rejoice. Amen.

Forgotten Gifts

Continue steadfastly in prayer,
being watchful in it with thanksgiving.
COLOSSIANS 4:2 ESV

It doesn't take long for something new to lose its shine and novelty. Whether it's a new outfit, a sleek car, or the perfect house, eventually the initial excitement fades, and the buyer becomes accustomed to and familiar with the purchase.

Unfortunately, this same tendency applies to blessings as well. God fulfills our deepest needs, provides jobs, heals sicknesses, gives peace and guidance, and grants us daily provisions and comforts. However, in the midst of life's hustle, it's easy for these undeserved gifts to go unacknowledged and unappreciated. God's blessings, whether monumental or miniscule, might, in time, begin to seem ordinary and unimpressive. And if these gifts are treated as rights that are deserved and these supposed rights go unsatisfied, discontent will inevitably gather in the spirit, poisoning one's joy.

But believers are called to have a different perspective. If they open their eyes to the blessings around them—opportunities, family, friends, the chance to experience beauty, love, grace, and life—they will remember that everything was given to them by God through His wisdom and kindness. When they see all the times that God listened to their prayers and responded, they will feel the closeness of His presence in every area of their lives. By the simple act of gratitude, they can draw closer to Him. —HM

God, thank You for all that You've given me.
Help me not to lose sight of it. Amen.

Closer Than We Think

In abundance of counselors there is victory.
PROVERBS 24:6 ESV

When tough, life-changing decisions need to
be made, it sometimes seems as though God
retreats quietly into the clouds, evading our
prayers for direction and guidance. Desperate
for reassurance and unsure of the next step, it's
easy to begin to read too deeply into normal
circumstances or to begin to see signs in
commonplace things. And from these supposed
revelations, people might receive contradicting
answers or solutions that defy common sense,
which draws them even deeper into confusion
and doubt.

Although God does reveal His will in uncon-
ventional ways, one of His best mouthpieces
is people. Decisions about education, careers,
marriage, childrearing, and where to live don't
have to be made alone. Discussing the situation

and praying with others is a wise way of deciding which path to take. God has placed specific people in our lives for a reason. He didn't mean for us to live in solitude with only a pros and cons list to consult. He wants us to be surrounded by a vibrant, diverse community of people who are willing to listen and share their own experiences and knowledge. So when it seems like God is silent and uninterested in your life, remember that He might be speaking through the people who are closest to you. — HM

God, thank You for revealing Yourself in so many different ways. Help me to find wise counselors to confide in. Amen.

A note from one of the authors:

Mothers and daughters share many things. DNA, mannerisms, jewelry, lipstick. In my case, my mother and I share a passion for writing. Even in my journal as an eleven-year-old, I wrote that my biggest dream was to be a writer—just like my mom. It seems she unwittingly passed the writing gene down to me.

But more importantly, my mom brought me up in the teachings and truths of Jesus Christ. She taught me that I have nothing to fear with God by my side and that He is only a prayer away. From her guidance, I learned about the incredible grace available to everyone through Jesus.

Our writing styles may be different, but we praise and love the same God. And I'm grateful that my first attempt at writing is with my mother.

Hillary McMullen